shape your eyes by shutting them

MINGLING VOICES
Series editor: Manijeh Mannani

Give us wholeness, for we are broken.
But who are we asking, and why do we ask?
            —Phyllis Webb

Mingling Voices invites the work of writers who challenge boundaries, both literary and cultural. The series issues a reminder that literature is not obligated to behave in particular ways; rather, it can defy convention and comfort and demand that readers summon the courage to explore. At the same time, literary words are not ordinary words, and the series implicitly raises the question of how literature can be delineated and delimited. While Mingling Voices welcomes original work—poems, short stories, and, on occasion, novels—written in English, it also acknowledges the craft of translators, who build bridges across the borders of language. Similarly, the series is interested in cultural crossings, whether through immigration or travel or through the interweaving of literary traditions themselves.

Series Titles

Poems for a Small Park
E.D. Blodgett

Dreamwork
Jonathan Locke Hart

Windfall Apples: Tanka and Kyoka
Richard Stevenson

Zeus and the Giant Iced Tea
Leopold McGinnis

Praha
E.D. Blodgett

The Metabolism of Desire:
The Poetry of Guido Cavalcanti
Translated by David R. Slavitt

kiyâm
Naomi McIlwraith

Sefer
Ewa Lipska, translated by Barbara Bogoczek and Tony Howard

Spark of Light: Short Stories by Women
Writers of Odisha
Edited by Valerie Henitiuk and Supriya Kar

Kaj Smo, Ko Smo /
What We Are When We Are
Cvetka Lipuš, translation by Tom Priestly

From Turtle Island to Gaza
David Groulx

Unforgetting Private Charles Smith
Jonathan Locke Hart

Shape Your Eyes by Shutting Them
Mark A. McCutcheon

shape your eyes by

Mark A. McCutcheon

eyes by

Poems

shutting them

AU PRESS

© 2019 Mark A. McCutcheon
Published by AU Press, Athabasca University
1200, 10011 – 109 Street, Edmonton, AB T5J 3S8

doi:10.15215/aupress/9781771992695.01

Cover image: Detail of painting by Hieronymus Bosch, *The Garden of Earthly Delights*
(ca. 1480–1505, Spain).
Cover design by Natalie Olsen, kisscutdesign.com
Interior design by Sergiy Kozakov
Printed and bound in Canada

Library and Archives Canada Cataloguing in Publication

Title: Shape your eyes by shutting them: poems / Mark A. McCutcheon.
Names: McCutcheon, Mark A., 1972– author.
Series: Mingling voices.
Description: Series statement: Mingling voices
Identifiers: Canadiana (print) 20190170549 | Canadiana (ebook) 20190170565
ISBN 9781771992695 (softcover) | ISBN 9781771992701 (pdf)
ISBN 9781771992725 (Kindle) | ISBN 9781771992718 (epub)
Classification: LCC PS8625.M33 S53 2019 | DDC C811/.6—dc23

We acknowledge the financial support of the Government of Canada for our publishing
activities and the Canada Council for the Arts, which last year invested $153 million to
bring the arts to Canadians throughout the country. Assistance is also provided by the
Government of Alberta through the Alberta Media Fund.

For Heather

Contents

Donne aux rêves que tu as oubliés la valeur de ce que tu ne connais pas.
                —André Breton and Paul Éluard, *L'Immaculée Conception*

Characters and voices in these stories began in what is real, but became, in fact, dreams.
                —Jayne Anne Phillips, *Black Tickets*

To win the energies of intoxication for the revolution—this is the project about which Surrealism circles. ... The reader, the thinker, the loiterer, the flâneur, are types of illuminati just as much as the opium eater, the dreamer, the ecstatic. And more profane.
                —Walter Benjamin, "Surrealism: Last Snapshot of the
                European Intelligentsia"

In the first class that I took, a class about theory, the teacher told us about the works of the novelist Juan Goytisolo. "Goytisolo uses plagiarisms (other texts) in several ways: sometimes his characters read, discuss, or see other texts. Sometimes two simultaneous texts compose the narrative. Sometimes Goytisolo changes someone else's text in an attempt to contaminate and subvert something or other. Count Julian, I mean Goytisolo, subverts, invades, seduces, and infects all that's abhorrent to him by transforming the subject into an empirical self, a text among texts, a self that becomes a sign in its attempt at finding meaning and value. All that is left is sex alone and its naked violence."
                —Kathy Acker, *My Mother: Demonology: A Novel*

Poetry can only be made out of other poems.
                —Northrop Frye, *Anatomy of Criticism*

Shadows the words

How old is your ardour?
Everything feels afterwards
and if echoes are shadows
the words in the storm
have no word for ocean, but if you live here
Eventually the birds become
record player. Electric & spinning.

Three votive candles

1. The angel answers: *The Holy Spirit will come upon you.*

She always has to be on top, or I'd break her wings beneath her on the bed. The condoms she brings from Heaven glow, faintly, and play ambient *alleluias*. With stainless steel fingernails she carves the Beatitudes on my back.

Blessed are they which do hunger.

And the sweat at the nape of her neck reeks of God's eternal sorrow. Her diamond nipples cut me into stained glass. I kiss her secret wings, and taste the ghost of a snail glazed in honey. When she comes, her halo explodes, and my mouth fills with feathers.

In the morning, I wake from Presbyterian dreams to pick platinum pubic hairs from the damp sheets. I hang one between my fingers like a fish hook of mercy.

2. Quoth Lesions of Nazareth: *Let suffering children come into me.*

The haemorrhage prophet was a fisher of mud. For forty days in the desert
he suffered the reptiles to come into him. In Galilee, he turned the loaves
to blisters. In the Decapolis, he flayed a mongrel hound. From Bethsaida to
Gennesaret, he walked on the wafers. The stigmata of palms weeping iodine,
yeast of Herod's immaculate infection. The haemorrhage prophet bit the eyes of
his disciples and burned the temple to a silhouette. He went with his truncheon
to assault a leper in the garden of Gethsemane. Transfigured, he emerged
wearing a swine's head.

The haemorrhage prophet died so that men would have eternal meat.

They brought him to Golgotha, where from a chalice he picked ten fresh
foreskins and ringed his fingers. He carried his own skull to the intersection of
wood. He inhaled the nails, he gnawed the cross.

Eli, Eli, the llamas spoke of *sabachthani.*

3. Whispers the prophet: *If you hear my voice and open the door, I will come in to you.*

After she married, Scheherezade kept her owls in the ovens of devotion. The ants in her husband's beard threw rice to the dog. In the bedroom closet, eyes rolled like wet marbles. In spring, cinnamon fell from the trees in red clouds.

Are you talking about the happy spider? he asked. He let his beard fill up with lice, and stayed up late eating Buddha rice.

On the front lawn, aliens from Paradise taught one another to pose in vogue freezeframe, still as the sculpted voluptuary Madonna. The dog cried.

Any questions? she asked. He was salting the television. *I'm afraid all my bondages are out rubbering the town red tonight. But your airplane stays relevant to the good china.*

In the back yard, the willows picked up their green skirts and slouched towards the windows. Among the branches, vultures knocked their circumcised skulls together in time. The willows watched as she shrouded him in scarves of sixty-watt light. In the living room, their love fidgeted before the ultraviolet shadows on the wall, squirming like a child who wasn't sorry.

Have I been whitelisted? she wondered.

Fifty more

o sweet mystery of life at last I've found youuuuu
sings Grandma to the cake as she dabs its rim
of cadaver wax icing

Grandpa comes back from the bathroom where
the pot roast and rat poison he'd eaten had
argued vehemently

the birthday boy their boy your dad has put up with you
for roughly half his life sentence
Grandma cuts the cake into a star

everyone holds out a paper plate begging for a Geiger counter
to the birthday boy you toast raising your spiced clam bifocals
here's to fifty more

at which Dad groans smiling or is it wincing punctuated by the
just audible rattle you might make if the trailer home door
were to open just then and Glenn Gould

were to walk in flanked by two showgirls in swimsuits
in Gould's left hand a dangling bikini top
in his right hand a freshly rinsed brain

prompting Grandpa to complain
what a horse's ass of a time
all this has been

Here is where was

Here a blue heron glides, wings wide, over the face of Sparrow Lake, the face of the lake glistening under the sun like crumpled foil, flattened by a child's open palms. Here an osprey brushes sunfish from the lake's green, ungroomed hair. Hear the late Canadian National rail wail away across the water, its line defining the horizon coniferous. Hear the campers sing the nonsense song we teach them—*lots of clouds move the mountains, and the water's full of stars*—to erase the songs that made less sense a century ago.

Where our fathers, rampant forebears and raw-winded ghouls, licked here down to its lichen-coated bones—*what lips it had were tattered and bloody*—bit open the rocky spine here and burned it black, whose fires fed on toxic marrow their tongues coaxed from deep stones, who cut their rough tongues on this shield asking *where is here*, who loosed here a strife of starlings, who evicted the loon, who left us this bereft new world whose true name now drops from the mandibles of bees on antibiotics.

Where the campers call the canoe-tripping river *The Caché*. Were you to tell Er that name sounds incongruous, urbane, she would tell you the river's real name, *Kosheshebogamog*. Where nobody anymore knows what that means. Where dragonflies bite each other in half. Where you say nothing without waving a pair of pine branches for antennae, without learning the redwing blackbird's song, spilling like rain over stony rapids, without canonizing the mosquito, without dreaming of fire when you sleep in your tent. *Where is here? Here was beauty and here was nowhere.*

Here it's not the silence that unravels you, it's the Babel of ten thousand untranslated tongues. So here forage for found syntax, here tune your sap-sticky antennae to hear the frequency of cicadas, here chart new constellations among the soft strobe of fireflies, here teach the campers that, to capture the flag, both teams must wear red. Here come home to your patience, like a mantis climbs a railway tie. Here give your love to the mosquitoes. Your stolen blood strafes the sky.

Second of the night

in the red rooted bed her sleeping hand
holds down your yearning shoulder
in counterpoint to her rocksteady breath
her reattached finger taps your skin
softly telegraphing a report from her dreaming

she builds the towering three-storey woman
between the dream home's floors
in the attic bathroom shine the eyes hair and shoulders
in the main floor kitchen fold the arms breasts and belly
in the cellar squat the hips calves and toes
each floor's segment held in a big black box

sleep is a timeshare where you lead a real
other life that dreams let you see so
who did you sleep last night moonlighting
as someone else say as the inspector of rows
of rain-damp rat-skin umbrellas blown inside out

No family one pictures

this couple came to Canada invented a fanning mill had it patented word came
the family had inherited some money if they went to claim it they never got
one pictures

Elizabeth born in 1867 never right in her mind broke her hip at eighty got
around at eighty-three broke her other hip and got around again the family
came by wagon mostly woods had to clear land to crop mother was opposed to
whiskey very plentiful in
how one pictures

William accidentally shot out hunting very sick at time of writing this trouble is
inherited and there is no cure have a coffin made to order Milton run over by a
wagon on a gangway no family
pictures the angel of

Christopher killed by a train opening a track switch died in a train-truck collision
the marriage didn't work riding a bicycle to work talking to a friend in a truck fell
under the front wheel Emma took a stroke lived long Dr. John a widow married
late had no family
how one pictures the angel

Charles a graduate injured his back never taught school TB and double
pneumonia at the last and his mind gone John cancer of the bone found dead
in bed a heart condition after a long illness twins born but didn't live died
suddenly after bed they have no family
history

Earl drowned in harvest time water went out of this pond after and never refilled
rheumatic fever John a policeman farmed had a grocery story and telephone
central a pool room and general story
of history

Cora Dolena married Francis died in 1947 kicked in the head by a runaway horse Francis is an installer for Bell Cora married again Allin got around fair for months before he died suffered how one pictures the angel of history

Grand parenthesis

Stuff the mattress with wings of ducks
Try to sleep in the rye-flavoured dusk
If you can't sleep, just think of somewhere you really liked to be
Stare at the ceiling until the stucco blows cloud figures
Wonder why they have fed you to the Hardy Boys
Over your head squirrels tumble through the attic rafters
The bedside basin, porcelain monstrance poised on a tea towel, smells of locust love
Wonder at the snakes outside your window
Wonder why everything takes longer for you
Snakes wing through the summer swamp air
Snakes whose mouths meal mayflies, smash moths
By the front door his rain boots wait for you and tomorrow
And tomorrow among the mourning doves
you take a stick to the fields
poke at steaming meteors of earth
point at crows, at orioles the colour of Hallowe'en
Now the walls begin to spin
and sleep smashes through the window
snapping you up in its fine teeth

And tomorrow
a green pasture ringed with conifers overgrown like the mouldering spines of giants
in back-fifty hems the evergreens stitch the land in this new morning after
Grandpa and you stand on the hill
his grey furred neck softly ruffed with gills
(He slept outside last night, the dew settling on his chill skin)
Cows coloured like chessboards amble the pastures, digesting
the hair of the land still green on their lips
The sparrows stay out of sight, their uneven whistle piping a lift into this morning after
Grandpa and you watch the sudden aurora strike this Easter sky
On the horizon, a row of new fires plume
alternative, historic suns

Above their white heat, the smoke skeins of older explosions rime the red clouds
Grandpa looks at you with eyes like fossils stolen from an empty beach
What now? you want to ask him
but he would ask you the same question
From a hundred miles away
the morning fires burn the tongues out of your staring heads
The cattle graze, indifferent to the fusing sky

Where the area code ends

after they say goodnight and turn out the light tiptoe
to the stairs to sit and listen as they talk and watch TV
wonder whether they know you sit crouched up here
waiting for them to shed their humanskin costumes

wake up in the bedroom with the safari curtains closed
on the backyard night against the overpass lights
to get out of bed plant your foot far from the bedside
out of reach of the mantislike claws waiting beneath

wander this suburban townhouse alone tonight
in the kitchen three stairs lead only into the wall
in the living room across from the split-log sofa
goldfish drift in the TV

on the upstairs landing opposite the chockablock closet
a black velvet painting tall as dad depicts an ostrich
the paint shimmers and creeps it's made of iridescent insects
carpeting the canvas this living painting never looks
the same way twice but the ostrich's eye always follows you

in this townhouse take comfort the cutlery has no eyes
and the aquarium harbours shells fish can hide in to die
in this townhouse the bedroom closets hide puppets
who have murdered their masters

behind mom and dad's bedroom closet door
a shaggy blue puppet grunts as he lifts weights
hush don't let it know you're alone in the house
but you trip over the butterfly net on the floor
and that puppet slams open the bedroom door

he always slams open the bedroom door chases you
around the house always corners you upstairs
in your parents' bedroom where you always open
the window and jump out looking up as you fall

in the sky float severed ears and out the dwindling window
that puppet howls at you as you plummet
not down your house's two storeys but the endless wall
of an apartment tower from which you fall and fall and

wake up in the bedroom with the safari curtains closed
hop away from the bed to evade what lies beneath
wander the house alone tonight and every night
in the kitchen again the three nowhere stairs

in the living room you hide behind the split-log sofa
while mom and your sister have tea with the neighbours
do not have tea with them all their heads are prunes
their mouths are puckered sphincters
they converse unintelligibly but with horrific politeness

wander this suburban townhouse you call home
where the area code ends between Metro Toronto
before the GTA and Markham before the grow ops
wander this townhouse alone tonight and every night

the nightmare always replays you lose count of its rehearsals
the house forever changes sets the sets bend the props warp
the tiny actors come and go through the wire that commutes
from the TV to the world outside

as the safari animal curtains damp the highway onramp lights
past the backyard in the night over a home you can only tell
apart from the others on the same street as the end unit
once you went to the Tanakas next door
their house your house turned backward
like you had walked through a mirror

that suburb where the area code ends like all suburbs
squatting on homeless native land on prime arable land
hatching a labyrinth of lookalike parallel worlds
subdividing into hives of tiny homes and inside each
all the closets teem with rattling red-legged locusts

Found and lost

While renovating our postwar bungalow,
under a kitchen floorboard we found a fifty-
year-old cache: cash, a pen, and a spiralbound
diary, whose writer had hidden this lifeline
from her husband, a battering drunk,
as the tiny pages cramped with cursive told us
over and over like a scratched record
broken with calls to her daughter
driven from that bad abode and feared lost;
and the cash was for her, and we saved
these things to give her, if you see her.

Take forever just a minute

Liver failure, said the specialist,
following months of my mother's mystery
pain, fatigue, and headaches no acetaminophen
or glass of water would banish.
Mom's name barely caught the bottom rung
of one long shaking ladder of a waiting list.

For long yellowing months she sat among company
like a sepia photo fading, slyly asking Dad
I'd like a smoke, or *A glass of white*, which he gently denied.

Dad stayed by her side day and night, he told me over the phone;
the bungalow became a palliative parlour, the hi-fi once
victoriously loud—with the Gibbs, Timmins, and Twain

(at our reception she'd sprung that disc on my new husband
I paid for this wedding, she ordered, *play "Feel Like a Woman"*
and dance with me, and flung him around the floor)

—now hushed, circled by nurses, her hours now shuttled
between her easy chair and the shuttered bedroom
where Dad sat watch and forgot how to sleep.

One May day after Dad's late call about the latest
ambulance trip, I locked the house, packed the kids,
drove east for three days, came to stay, to aid, to say goodbye,

found Mom paper-thin, bones shining through skin, every shift
from recliner to bed left a lighter dent in the upholstery.
She couldn't stand up by herself anymore.

Her name never rose one rung up the waiting list.
Her grandniece mailed a hinky get-well drawing of grave angels
praying for the heaven-bound; we never gave it to her.

I studied nurses slicing lavish helpings from their huge hearts.
I studied Dad's devotions, attentions, and insomnia.
I changed her, bathed her, soothed each surly furuncle,
served her prune spoonfuls, helped her pass stone-sharp stools.

I stole moments to eat an English muffin with peanut butter
(Mom's favourite snack); I encouraged my nervous daughters
to hold her hand and apprehend in these ways
the adult child's dues I had come to pay.

I tempered my ministrations with mercenary practicalities:
rifled a box of unworn jewellery, pilfered the emerald
earrings I'd given her one Mother's Day, replaced
them with the unwanted gallstone of recalling her call
my sister the *less difficult* daughter, and closed the box.

One night, suddenly upright, she stated, *Life isn't right*
a curse on fortune to count among her last words
which, eulogizing later, Dad guessed she'd meant *isn't fair*.
Another night, abruptly animate, she touched Dad's cheek,
said "Come to bed," which he gently declined, and they wept.

One day the kids and I came in to find the house flooded
by the Bee Gees' "More Than a Woman" in the living room.
Mom and Dad were dancing, twirling slowly as an LP in the
pollen-dust sunlight:

Their dance, more defiance than farewell, arrested the kids,
spared this poem from attending a funeral and played it a love song instead
—*we can take forever just a minute at a time*—
Their dance turned all of us who saw them into mute pillars of salt,
astonished at the sight of love on its last legs
still intent on turning the world under its sure step.

•

A sound outside the house

It's after eleven, the kid's asleep, hopefully she's driving home from her shift by now, you're scribbling on the hot laptop at the kitchen table messy with placemats paper and crumbs, you hear a sound outside the house, like the yard gate banging open, you wait to hear her turn her key in the side door, but nothing, she doesn't turn her key in the side door, the wind picks up now, that sound outside wasn't the gate, was a different bang, was it upstairs, the wind wheezes through the elm branches, you weren't expecting rain until tomorrow, maybe the sound was the rain not the gate, you go to the living room window, part the curtains to see if it's raining, if she's parking, but it's not raining, she's not there, the wind bends over the election sign that pins down the lawn, a hare bolts from the green shadows around your neighbour's dim house across the street, running straight for your house, no, not a hare, a white cat, running at the light spilling through the split drapes, at your face in the window, you don't know this cat, it's got no collar, close the drapes quickly, fear splashes you, cold as cloudburst rain, if it's really not raining, if that cat weren't wearing the kid's face, if the gate's not banging again.

A pantoum to smash pandas

for an anxious nine-year-old

this infection mimics your molecules so antibodies attack your own brain
this technique attacks the immune system disguised like a lie paralyzing the victim
your own brain keeps tricking you tripping a false alarm you can't disable
hostage to this impostor all you can do is fret over vectors and wash your hands

this technique attacks your immune system its style is a lie paralyzing the victim
stuck at the sink thinking your hair touched the toilet seat or your pants
hostage to this impostor all you do is worry about germs and wash your hands
scrub your hands until they're red and raw and your classmates ask you why

stuck in the bathroom asking if your hair touched your pants or dipped in the toilet
following a false alarm's direction makes as much sense as arguing with an infection
scrub your hands until they bleed and in class your unclean friends ask why
maybe you touched your pants maybe they touched the toilet but so what

to follow a false alarm's instruction is as illogical as arguing with an infection
you can't touch your pants your hair you don't want to worry can't live like this
maybe you touched your pants maybe splashed urine on them but again so what
when you touch your pants but don't wash your hands that's how you beat this

you can't touch your pencils your puzzles you don't want to worry you can't live
you can't do anything you just want to be happy you ask to go to the hospital
when you touch your pants but don't wash your hands that's how you defeat this
remind yourself you're more than your worries they're not more than you

you can't do anything you just want to be yourself again to go to the hospital
tell yourself this is the last time but you said that last time you can't help it
remember you're bigger than your fears they're not bigger than you
you flinch at gnats now but recall at Tikal you were first to handle a tarantula

tell yourself this is the last time did you say that last time can you help it
this infection mimics molecules making your antibodies battle your own brain
you flinch at gnats but recall Tikal where you were first to handle that tarantula
your brain's mimic tricks you tripping a false alarm can you can we talk it down

Anthropocene obscene as orange

all the news is weather now and haze the new azure
every sky now the sky of Rousseau's *Nègre attaqué par un jaguar*:
a pustulant slate pinned by a pestilent sun
as fittingly orange as fake tans and falling tamarins
quand le ciel est toujours orageux, orange is the new blue
the last colour humans learned will be the first they forget
as smog and fallout forever pall the sky's former nitrogen hue
the new orange sun estranges all that hinges on its glower

smoke is the new wind and forest fires filter the light you see all
through like algorithms filter all the news that's fit to squint
like all-weather news this pervasive smoke aches your head
like reading *the Red Cross is grateful for your gift to Hurricane Irma*
wording that makes you wonder where your money's going
in this drowning world read up on storm surges and listen
with refreshed attention to the best of REM
the cities wash away
eye of the hurricane listen

and to the Hip whose *New Orleans is sinking* turned into fact too
contemplate how weather cuts the power of the state
the smoke-smuggered sky decants another uncanny rain
so close your conflict mineral laced laptop and prep your go bag
take just what's irreplaceable like letters and photos
memorize the less busy back country routes the radius
of available mileage and never go to sleep on an empty tank
but whether you'll need to drive or to dig depends on what
outages and outrages the orange day after tomorrow brings

Room for one more

on night shifts I run blood
samples from the 2nd floor Cardiac unit
to the lab in the basement

one night waiting on 2 for the elevator I watched
its 3 lit long enough as if called I heard its doors open
and close but it opened empty on 2 as I stepped in

the next night as I waited cradling patient blood vials
the elevator stopped opened and closed on 3 and
on 2 opened empty or with nobody I could see

this *multo* mischief went on all month
I took to the stairs a longer dimly lit walk down
cinderblock halls hearing more than one pair of feet

I asked the Charge if I could send the samples by tube
(the hospital's pneumatic courier system)
but glass is too fragile

I hurt my back no more stairs back into the elevator
just me and who or what from 3
in a big tube sucked down through the walls

as liable to smash as a blood vial crimsoning
the insides of the hospital walls dank with iron stink
dripping rot and clot and shadows like all our tubes do

so every night the walls suck the elevator up and down
and to let me and who knows what else in
the lift still just stops like any heart will

The leaf is not the line

On the first day up the Inca Trail you ask Vincente if America campaigns
contra coca in his country. The people won't abide it, he says:
la hoja de coca no es droga, no plague on Toronto's toilet-top choppers.
So much coca is needed, Vincente says, and so many chemicals to
make just a little cocaine, there's no comparing the leaf and the line.
More like *manzanilla*: a balm against the beating migraine of mountain
sickness; a subtle appetite suppressant and laxative; a protein-rich pick-me-up.
It's the perfect trail mix, you joke, as you buy a bag from a quiet trailside vendor
(blithely overpaying, but when will you come to Peru again).
And a natural dentifrice, your newlywed adds with politesse, to go
by all the *campesinos'* bright smiles. In the villages you pass they pose
for photos; the walls of small shops bear big billboards for American colas,
while distant hillsides bear patches scorched bare to form words, which
Vincente translates: candidates' slogans for the upcoming election.
The coca leaf gleams dark army green above, its pattern of veins like
the back of your hand, and beneath, it's the gentle yellow of open avocado.
The leaf in the mouth first feels tough as card, then softens like lamb's ear.
How thinly live those who never try anything once.
(On your last night in Lima you eat a roasted guinea pig.)
Coca tastes of dusty jasmine tea lightly honeyed, or freshly mown lawn
laced lightly with iodine. Its scent suggests knowledge
as old as the Cordillera Blanca, as ancient as the snake.
You chew it continually up the Trail's endless ascent,
Vincente noting those stretches of Trail rebuilt after quakes for us tourists,
across the four-thousand-foot-high saddle of Dead Woman's Pass,
across the cloud canopy cusp of the Amazon headwaters,
the Quechua guides racing past you and your drumming headache
with khaki duffels on their backs and only sandals on their bare bleeding feet.
On your second day at Sayaqmarka, Vincente tells you archaeologists
unearthed a girl sacrificed and mummified, in her
stomach a last meal of enough coca to numb her nerves, but not enough

to get anywhere as high as the DEA crop dusters that fly so unlike condors
over Bogotá's backyards and the plazas of La Paz, indiscriminately bathing
ambassadors and schoolchildren alike in cloying herbicidal rain.
Absent America's paltry, toxic ideas, stuck like chewed gum in the deep pockets
of the so-called war on drugs (which means two things),
you might have brought your bag home; you later learn some of your fellow
travelers did, undeclaring. But you leave it with Vincente.
How anyone can acclimatize to Peruvian altitudes you'll never know.
The night before you reach Machu Picchu, the Irish guy in your group,
Martin, sings "Old Man River" like he was Paul Robeson,
his improbable bass voice circling the campfire like a puma.

Why the blue whale risked its neck

Blue whales descended from pre-Socratic philosophers
who walked to the sea, dropped their papyrus,
shed their robes and waded into the waves
under an ancient Aegean sun.
Naked they swam, grabbing the sea's shoulders
that bore them out to open water,
the brine brushing off their spindly limbs and digits.
The wine dark waves wore away neurotic details
like earlobe and eyebrow, ponytail and fingernails,
and divisive necks, which the water pressed until
they telescoped in, reminded by their bodies
that the body is the mind.
Their quarrelsome cocks retracted like claws,
leaving scars on thickening skin
worn down to bare life in bright thought.
Their fervid brains gradually cooled
as they graduated down the stone-heavy
ocean depths, ponderously navigating stoic icebergs,
inductive kelp jungles, the sophistry of kraken and shark,
floating for days in contemplation.
As they inhaled clouds of krill and cynic plankton,
they translated dialectic into dialects
of sonorous bellow and squealing eureka,
folding logic like origami lobsters
to festoon the vast hulls of their heads.
Submarine hulks of random excess reverie
submerged in discipline's purity, pure as distilled
hemlock, pure as harpoons.

Mab and Burke

—My name's Burke. Mab spat in Burke's eye. In the field the other boys played soccer.
—My name's Burke, he told Mab, putting the tissue back in his pocket.
—I'm Mab. They chased each other until Mab had Burke pinned under his knees. Rain spat on their backs and faces. Laughing, they were dragged to the office of the hockey-faced principal.

—Hey, look. A dead rabbit.
—We should bury it.
—Fuck that, Burke. Find a stick.

Burke came out of the operating room feeling like the minister of arachnids. Each hand now waved just two broad fingers over the thumb. Each digit lined with sticky pads for climbing walls like a fly. He sat in the waiting room ripping ads out of *Time* while Mab's operation finished. Now and again Burke heard a drill whine, a saw growl through bone, a sharp *pnk!* of steel thread getting snipped.

Mab came out into the waiting room, and Burke went blind for five years.

In Burke's most embarrassing dream, his dad coached him in sex lessons with his mom in a drab, shabby motel room. In Mab's most embarrassing dream, he sucked his own cock. This is also Mab's favourite dream.

One night at Mab's house they played *Thriller* over and over and became captains of warring star fleets. *For no mere mortal can resist.* After annihilating galaxies and each other's alien hordes, they got bored. What pubescent boy hasn't puppeted his penis to make its little lips ape speech? Mab's mother shouted down at them from upstairs. Burke smothered Mab in the sofa, the funk of forty thousand years sighing from its crevasses.

Mab rose up. Under the black branches of an ash tree Burke has been Cained. The arrow in his eye bites the trunk behind his head. Burke's head is a gyroscopic puddle.

They'd been shooting at crows in the park. A park employee drove up in a golf cart and told them they couldn't practice archery in a public park. So they went away until he drove off. Mab is a good archer. But now Burke must teach the alligators of penitence to dance faster.

The first crow Mab shot burst into blue flames and dropped to the field. The grass smoulders. The second crow Mab shot got pinned through its wing to a passing cloud. The third crow Mab shot was hiding behind Burke's optic nerve. Now he sees only charcoal feathers.

L'âme de l'homme est fait du papier

Paper Kid haunts the locker-lined hall, all crumple and shred inside.
Crow-coloured clouds overcast her heart. The sun's tawny tongues lick the
cinderblock walls. Some lockers loll open, many more closed, cool as coffins.
Paper Kid angles past these shrines to shoegaze, sweat, and other kinds of
kindling. Crisp and slight as letterhead she slips around doorjambs, vanishes in
profile. Her sneakers squeak and stutter.

Up the hall ahead, a classroom door opens and and Glass Girl walks out,
glittering as moonlit snow. She touches the sun-warmed wall, smiles as wide as
an errant rabbit spilled across the road by careless cars. Paper Kid sees Glass
Girl, notes she's wearing her political lipstick. Paper Kid, compelled, chases her
in slow motion, crinkling like carbon copy with want. The long window at the
end of the hall overlooks the dead-grass playing field, has twelve tall panes, and
twenty-two housefly husks on its sill. Paper Kid follows Glass Girl, watching her
walk like an artless underwater waltz. The kid picks up her pace, starts to glow
like eucalyptus in the furnace of the excommunicated century. Starts to burn,
slow, an ant under glass. That arsonist, lust, lights her shoelaces, her shirtcuffs,
her eyelashes. In the slipstream behind Glass Girl's stride, Paper Kid steps faster,
drinking the summer-beach scent of her silicon skin.

Glass Girl turns down the stairs and Paper Kid can't stop herself any more than
an oceanfloor flatworm can stop itself getting trawled up to the surface. The
gridded wide window yawns ahead at the end of the hall. Paper Kid's arms curl
like news clippings. Consumed, immolated, immaculate, she crashes headfirst
through the window. Black flakes float and scatter into the still indifferent April
skies.

A murmuration of ash starlings drifts down to the dead grass. Where Glass Girl
soon steps, softly, coolly, and fleeting as a midsummer momentary rainfall.

Voyager 2, thinking, types things

Very very very very very small
Billion miles recalculating
We don't know details well at all
The direction we were last going

Calculable but undetectable
Earth would be the one-yard line
As bright planets are invisible
Now does not exist in space-time

Outer solar system missions
With the winds from other stars
As in trigintillion years never

But please do send invitations
People might think there are bears
To hear from you by tomorrow over

Lunar sonata

weird music heard the radio
crew the moon through headsets
whether or not it was 1969

orbit out of radio contact
nobody can hear the public
knew everything the mission
went unexplained unsettling
music through the module
like they never heard space
that whistling hour
regained radio control

to think noise should be logic
if something recorded then
there was science
withhold the public in
the public's interest

hear anything years
old memory making up something
you really know if you're the moon
and hear weird noise from Earth
what could you think

tapes have been available
digital archives questioned
television told that incident
interference something other

who flew in space heard wonder
pin down proof different
transcripts and transmissions
check your correction
version this question
lost and declassified
sound these changes

Baby Bee explains Jupiter's Great Red Spot

the insects are all at war
see the blue
thousands of dragonflies
see the red
millions of ladybugs
see the white
billions of moths
see the black
that's where the photographers get in
it's a planet made of fighting flesh
they're all competing
for the dragons
who rejoice in the meadow

Whose eyes are shut in every photo

this girl gets digital privacy she hunts
alone rolling absence down stairs and
cleaning up after the spiders and
strafing the countryside with accidental
content and skyscraper pearls

under the counter-surveillance duvet
her many arms larval stamp with wants
can you hear the radishes roll around
in the darkness of the net
needs that don't transmit via email

we'd like to get her into odd job securities
like laser hair or liquid heirlooms or
esotropia futures or ergonomic harp stools
we'd like her to ignite whatever meadow she
wants we'll be calling if she hasn't

figured out how her rainbows
hunt on two point million hectares
we fear someday someone's going to
run the sun out of her and she'll write
that dream will haunt us all down

Heaven help the roses

For Pauline Davis, a.k.a. "the Peace Lady," 1943–2017

Toronto knew her as the Peace Lady:
For hours she'd stand athwart an overpass
That spanned the Parkway through the Don's ravine;
On Steeles, on Finch, on Lawrence, Eglinton.
She wore a white robe, her brown hand held high;
Two fingers telegraphing, simply, *Peace.*
When driving past we'd roll the windows down
And wave *Peace* back as Dad tapped on the horn.
At school we traded true Peace Lady facts:
She lived near the river, she kept raccoons.

In *Nineteen Eighty-Four*, cold war scares raged.
In Sunday school, we read *When the Wind Blows.*
Our seventh-grade science teacher confessed
Where he'd wish to be if the bomb got dropped
On Toronto: "Directly beneath it."
In English we read Wyndham's *Chrysalids.*
On TV, Muppets sang "Can't we be friends?"
Max Headroom unearthed radioactive waste
And several times a day the networks played
Emergency broadcasts, as grey and dark
As Reagan and Chernenko, null and void
As country roads shown in *The Day After.*

One night the evening news displayed how wide
A circle of fallout would spread in case
An ICBM struck the city's core.
That circle's edge—that emptied area code—
Engulfed our neighbourhood. Sleepless that night,

I lay and pictured houses on my street
Intact but vacant, windowless, and still,
All marred with carbon shadows, disused toys.
The air a thick green, toxic algae bloom,
Through which survivors shuffled, half melted,
Like plastic action figures burned by kids.

Through nervous years she graced our roads with peace,
A figurehead of hope on Toronto's
Concrete prow; but when the millennium turned,
When cold war turned to market war, and we
Put movie studios in our pockets,
She feared they made her mission a new threat.
She was weaponized as mass distraction,
As drivers courted carnage in pursuit
Of perfect shots. So she stood down, gave up
The call for all to bid farewell to arms.

"The 'state of emergency' in which we
Live is not the exception but the rule,"
Warned Benjamin, through 1940's storms.
I want the news to tell us Pauline won,
That she got a Nobel or the Order
Of Canada, or has been canonized.
Made statutory. Cast as stone icon
For all guerrilla artists to raise up
On all the city's bridges and highways,
A figurehead to help us navigate
To any year but 1984:
A year whose end we're all waiting for, still
As silhouettes burning to windowless walls.

Forgive me Cathy for

I have skinned my shin running through the heather
I have grimly picked at that wound further shunning antiseptics
until it raised a scar as sympathetic as your exquisite face that
I have ever had the pleasure of beholding incarcerated
in the locket you gave me that I have loyally worn like a leash
I have never confessed before but came close on exhuming your coffin Cathy
I have been down so long that when I first came to
the Heights a raw foundling you looked like up to me
I have been contemplating suicide but it really doesn't suit my style
I have always found myself determined to survive I have smoked one toke
over the line I haven't got the time time I have been a fool of kismet
I have sent stuffed bears to be rent by curs I have missed your tripwire wit
I have perused the daguerreotype albums of the beloved silvery dead
I have excellent aim I have to recollect the scent of your uncombed hair
I have torn from a bible the page that begets *In the beginning*
and eaten it before the besotted eyes of the faithful
I have to be in heaven by which I mean you Cathy I am Cathy
I have a dread of spreading civil unrest I have read more than you would fancy
I have suddenly realized the meaning of *My Mother: Demonology*
I have borne global warming while eating black pudding
I have no friends I have a dream I have to remind myself to breathe
I have to get you back you wick slip vixen hot and shocking as any siren
I have a right to kiss her only if she smiles just like you smiled
I have told my folks I'm getting help Cathy but I'm helpless before you
I have lapped musky rum from your quim I have some things to do
I have been thinking of our last night together when we lay
rain-stippled behind the low stone wall on the rentier's farm
in the cryptogamous country that claimed neither of us and
you climbed on me until your lips became my skin it was thirsty
I have masturbated imagining you in my dank bunk twice today already
I have absquatulated furtive as a sasquatch with pilfered porcelain and

bills from the shop's till but now I have but pennies to my mendicant name
I have just returned from a visit to my landlord I have come home let me
have it I have lost the locket I have just heard the branches scratch
the brittle window strobe-lit under bombastic thunder Cathy I am sorry
I have sinned against you if I spoke a false god's name not yours my dirty
deity how dare you leave me my confessions have not relieved me
have mercy lead me down to you I have to know Cathy what must I do
to haunt your ghost Cathy what haunts a ghost

Ever

        wherever lavender blooms
over blue savannahs   whenever hove to her
whether you warrant this windfall   her laughter

her touch   a tourniquet   a quiver   her divine whim
your dervish fervour her sinuous river shape ancient
fresh as water   her egret silhouette   her marten sense

hew whatever walls arrest you like   a law
refashion a fallow hovel into bare verdant heaven
better shelter from ever heavier weather

line your nest with equal parts matter and ether
leaven her summers with wander and feathers
cover her winters with ravens and glitter

        her love   your welter of penniless wealth
        your heart   a lit votive to heat her

The lineaments

in you wife
I would desire
what indoors is all haze
sound the lineaments
of gratified deep fire
these illicit
syllables

alone at the front desk
slide your hand
under your skirt
press fingers to lips
your swift slick digits
quicken a private rush
leave Reception blushing

after work wet as weather
you pin me to a park bench
your run-cut legs snug
around my hips as jets
fog the city we syncopate
the secret liquid funk
one pulse under two coats

contain my ardour
like a virus how
your body glows
firm and bright as vows
Monday moans or vowels
blossom from your throat
like nobody's business

New patriot love

on a red-letter day
in their nation of the bedroom
she and he fuck out a new flag
a Rorschach candy-cane splash
of semen and menses
hot with the swing beat of empire
with the gasp that sinewaves her French curve throat
with the groan that urges his Saxon lust
their bare monogamy prints this
new flag staining their woven skins
like a compass aches for north and heavy weather
no "owl kill in snow" this *Unifolié* frail and free
this flag homeless as the nativity
this flag identical with the fast
failing microstate it flies for

in the hinterland of their unboxed unsprung bed
in the unimagined community of their rented room
she and he stand and kneel and sway and slip
and on the wall amnesiac poppies stare black-eyed
at the poppies tattooing the field
of her narcotic back
as she glances
pushes back his plunging front
like mortar melting in foxhole
they forget themselves
they forget the forgetting that all flags demand
as the flag blurs and dries and prints the linens
as with glowing hearts they seethe rise
charge into each other
on guard for only each other
and so for all

You and you kiss the knife moon

on dimming decommissioned nights
of subways of marsh tower arrays
say the ozone layer is good
say radiological steam
through the window
the pink-veined sky of slugs
and your love turn hot and rotten
say beloved wash the flesh

the gift is a body of you
bathing with bathing with
your trunk as the gift is other
slack flesh from each other
beginning the mirror tantra
like everything mirrors
the vermillion she handfuls
written you lick sweat and lap honey

high strained hosts bite
open a thousand voyeur angels pink
light in a cloud each other
all the angels crack worms
take tender puzzled horns
over ecstasy watching red
mites swarm the woman you love
beloved soap and trees of sponge

you corpse cover each other
the moon sharpens her drops
glaciers map the woman you love

as the water has written
as sings the sidewalk
say your come traces mercury
the crimson rimmed corpse made
its horse rise in other flesh

dragonfly faces knead each other
through weed-choked dusting
you both and your and your coming
corrode fold each other
on the uranium floor
boiling you into glistening
loaves of salt skin amid plumes
blood by the freckled bathtub

for the night a city
fills the bathroom
you turned unwitting flutes
you and your secret ravines
you and you kiss the knife moon
tender and hard as mirrors
puzzled as any lovers taking
hold of the slow fluid night

Grosvenor Road

the last train rattles the windowpanes of your
run-down walk-up waking you to cats wailing
under the burnt car on Grosvenor Road
on your narrow bed the new woman stirs in sleep
sparks arc in the circuits of her narcoleptic hair

under the thin pillow shimmers a chrome blender
you drop your drowsy hand in
the steel claw slurries your fingers
on rails mirror bright under light pollution
the trains worm with their mates

the Islington sky swells a faceless eggplant
babies crawl under the burnt car's slashed tires
breathe in this woman's dreams like nicotine
lean over sleep's cliff face the choppy water below
dark as everything you can't know

this shared room's walls tilt towards the ceiling
fold your arm over her tender as a mantis talon
as sleep's undertow drags you down
you hold each other and you each hold others
tight as secrets in the swollen eggplant night

Shape your eyes by shutting them

Face the mirror
lift your thumbs to your eyes and
without pausing for thought
push them from their sockets
Exhale through the agony until
the quelling numb of shock
face the mirror take in your defacement:
your eyelids flaccid shells, red-rimmed
your upturned palms each bear
one blue eye, blood puddled
wonder what vision lets you witness this
wrap your eyes in a tissue
pocket them in case, but
where you're going, those broken eyes
will only blind you

In a wide wooden barrel she stands
knee deep in enucleated eyes
gathering her skirt around her thighs
she makes wine
stains her feet and calves pressing juice
from ten thousand and one visions
the brew breathes a bouquet reminiscent
of the farm yard on ram castrating day
asphalt and copper, sweat and water
she bows to dip and fill a long-stemmed glass
she passes it to you
the vintage swirls, murky as cider
made with last year's apples
in the meniscus float unfiltered irises
watching you drink

The space of one paragraph

Two hours ago she had sat up in bed, said *Make the words go away*. He woke, asked what she'd said. *I just want to sleep*, she said. In the bathroom he found pill bottles that hadn't been on the counter before when he'd brushed his teeth. The voice on the poison control line told him to inventory all she'd ingested. *Even the words?* Now he sits in the ICU waiting room trying to focus on the copy of *Maldoror* between the TV's blue flicker and the April lightning licking the windows. Nearby patients doze, watch TV, talk quietly: *Guess I'll get the papers and go home. Crows never follow you at least. I tell you there's no bridge that don't end in midair. It's like love was gravity not a hurt word.* The nurse comes over. *Want to see her, or are you good?* The nurse fish-eyes his book's cover: a gaunt man, mouth agape, struggles out of a coffin. In the patients' room, she sleeps on a cot, under a blanket the same blue as her pale blue eyes. The look on her sleeping face that of a trapped raccoon. Tear-carved creases trace her nostrils, the corners of her eyes. The IV drips something clear into her arm. Her lips and chin, stained black by the charcoal cocktail they'd fed her. Or has she been drinking ink again, *the fucking words*. Behind the door to the small bathroom he sees tile walls splashed with her nightmares, regurgitated, unpunctuated. Sentences sidewind down to the sewers, baptize blind reptiles, dark clots of signifiers swept off by subterranean rivers. She looks as light as a leaf on a puddle, raw as a frog skinned by dry prairie grass. Every colour in this room is a grey that goes on for miles: highway, newsprint, stormfront. Her closed eyes drugged past dreaming, but all she'd dreamt was fractal vortices of vomit. Whatever's dripping into her arm opens an umbrella under depression's mental monsoon. This is the third emergency hospital trip since they started dating, the second since they moved in together. Earlier today he'd clocked ten hours at the florist's, wrapping bouquets of Colombian carnations for corporate Mother's Day orders, the unventilated warehouse air cloyed by pesticide. A lizard tiny as his pinkie darted out of a box, got lost in the walls. She floats in a bed beyond hope, treading neurochemistry's heaviest water. He sits in a chair beyond exhausted. And quick as that lizard he knows he doesn't love her and can't tell her. Beyond the curtains other patients crouch, cornered by IV stands, telemetry screens, trays of baked steel, crates of spent syringes, boxes of ferrets nesting in wet red cotton. *Code indigo,* intones the intercom. When did he return to the waiting room? From the TV drifts a documentarist's dulcet voice: *These men are exploring a world never before seen by human eyes.* A bathyscaphe drifts down the blackest ocean. Its camera raptures the creatures of the ocean floor, creatures that move by pulsing, that resemble snowflakes or equations, their veins coursing with antifreeze not blood. Creatures who may get better or kill themselves, now or years from now, either way he can't bear to know. He picks at his fingernail quicks. *All we know about life in these depths of the ocean,* the documentarist says, *would barely fill the space of one paragraph.* As would anything he might write about the depths he's in. He closes his eyes, wants to walk out, hole up in the apartment, smoke weed and read about squids in flight and bowers of hermaphrodites until he can't tell whether he's awake or dreaming. Dark machines hum in the hospital basement. Near the ceiling perch unblinking birds. The faces of the quiet patients glow cathode blue.

Was I asleep?

Nive's driving as you leave downtown, headed for the sprawling wrecked suburbs. Abandoned agoras of burnt-out big box shops and crumbling business parks. The orange highway bisects the horizon, bordered by dark hulking factories whose thin chimneys plume needles of flame. Nive pulls off at a gas station; she gets out to pump. The only other car there is a blue rocket car, designed for breaking speed records, for reaching velocities that strip off its red and white racing stripes. Follow Nive into the cramped, dank gas station store.

On a long-ago bus ride into ancient Athens, you and Nive together at the back of the bus, sharing food and headphones; you pecked at her décolletage, mesmerized by the fine down between her breasts. The bus barrelled through diesel-choked streets, past pedestrians missing pieces of their faces, past the fallen Acropolis. Flocks of tick-riddled warblers dropping onto the roads where tires ground them into brown paste. As dusk bruised the sky, Nive started and said *Was I asleep? Because I just had the feeling that we're all going to die.*

In the beginning, everyone walked the highways that scar the city. Because you are sick of the dawn, no exit ramps or bridges invite you to appreciate their graffiti, survey their stone vistas. *Now comes the time who lives to see 't, that going shall be used with feet.* How depthless the darkness of a night without those strobes of red and white, heavy traffic's hazard lights. As you left downtown, three men sat under an overpass like trolls, one of them balancing an empty grocery cart on the edge of the exit lane. Beautiful as the chance encounter of a shopping cart with your passenger door.

The gas station store has one narrow aisle, its shelves stacked floor to ceiling with dusty junk and junk food. At the back sits a crow-haired woman. Nive pays the woman for the gas and they start chatting in Armenian. You go to the car. Out by the pump you meet the rocket car driver, a big guy who reeks of rye. In the rocket car cockpit reclines his little boy, who has a fever and can't speak. The man reaches down, turns his son over to show his sweaty back, on which three carved initials are scabbing over: *B.E.A.* The man says *When you sit with meat you rot.* Nive exits the store, comes over to you. The factories all still set fire to the soot-streaked sky. *Now where?*

The Pit of Carkoon

In this desert dwells a sarlacc, a ziggurat-shaped carnivore
broken stones surround its sandy lamprey lips
teeth like sapling-sized porcupine quills ring its vast maw
from the sphincter at the bottom of the pit
twin tongues lash out like bullwhips

Strewn around the sand
you'll find philosophers' hats, bottles, a sandal
all stones may be eaten
all lichens will grow both ways: forward and back in time
here under the sand green ferns grow

You should know
here to say the word *nowhere* brings comfort
for miles around the ravenous, stationary sarlacc
ostriches peer up like prairie dogs from their burrows
egg skulls bob atop their swaying sand-buried spines

Under the sand in the monster's cathedral stomach
thin feral babies shelter in ulcers repurposed as caves
they live on olive pits, distilled piss, severed toes
they object to the outside world on moral grounds

All nights become variations on a salt pan desert
occupied only by monsters and the dead
all deserts version the night, but under the sand
in the moist inhabited caves sweet ferns grow
you should know

Raver in the bathroom

in this hot throbbing bright box full of angels
the pharmasonic *frisson* of towering bass timbre and MDMA
gives way to that old base reminder so soldier
head to the head nearest the dance floor

kick open the door sweep for tweakers and random grue
if the floor floods no deeper than house then maybe you can even
the closing door damps the dub and you wade in watch
your step on the tile wonder what bug you contracted or can catch

hitch up your fat pants
that impractical fabric tub you bob about the party in
to keep the cuffs from sucking up what liquid funk
Pollocks the floor dank with vectors

the rave bathroom tests you to reckon how feckless
the pill and the pot and the tab have rendered you
how according to your hyperactive amygdala
any of a myriad missteps means exposure or even death

judge which urinal seems most commodious to staying
sanitary and station yourself past the splash zone
aim at one point an ice cube a hole a thrown roach
in the adjacent urinal a wet cellphone hums and waits for rust

great now a chatty doppelgänger two urinals over
dogs your relief rehashes the urban mythic nonscience
that metabolizing molly drains your spinal pith
whatever he says you just softeye his facial all skeletal

turn to the sink hope for hot water or at least soap
confront only one working tap cold and left running
all the soap dispensers yawn vandalized and depleted
but you find paper towels miraculously still dry

draw the brittle bottle from your pocket to refill it
don't let it touch the spittoon sink or rust-rimed faucet
as it fills face your sweat-drenched mug in the glass
your pupils open vast caverns in the corneas' red mesas

all the mammal vapour every body in this greenhouse offgasses
fogs the mirror in a glaze of glyphs or
roric Rorschachs ghosting the misty glass
letters names slurs curses smudged by cursive digits

driven to delirious scrivening by deals or other demons
evaporating articulations attest *S+J* or *RUN DNB*
or *kill me now* or just an Ozymandian name say *Mendoza*
the mirror maps you a palimpsest of scribbles and secretions

trip on your own gaze and apprehend this is the dose that will do for you
but until then you still have to carry water and remember the steps
and stretch a convincing face over the knot of skewed drives comprising you
and repeat these trips as infrequently as possible

an earful of tough naifs bursts into the bathroom
exit just as they enter and earn bonus points for not touching the door handle
one turns as you pass and his gaunt pallor shocks you but this is another mirror
ask yourself again what have you got what death have you caught

the crew pulls plastic packets from socks crotches and knitted coifs
they all pile into one highly suspect stall
after midnight the rave bathroom slips fast
from modern amenity into medieval miasma

bounce on beat out to the big room where you
let your cuffs scuff and spread whatever biohazard you now host
infecting all the tuned-in turned-on so-called humans
who turned up here to build a city for a night

Like opening your refrigerator door

> The Facebook experience is like opening your refrigerator door,
> staring in, not sure what you're looking for.
> —Dani Fankhauser, *Mashable*, 25 Jan. 2013

At the inaugural Jane Austen Janis Joplin Jubilee Ball now popping in Austin.
A refrigerator lolls on the diatomaceous sidewalk, dreaming in jellybeans, its
fingernails razor blades, its face your face. Ride your bike down sloughs of
cretaceous molasses that cascade across the forest canopy. Sing of the city on
the river where a plague of trout roils.

In the ashen webs of the refrigerator's deepest recess, goldfish flounder, glinting
like maple keys. Like all fish they flip their burned-off beaks in disgust, accosted
by the sight of your naked fins. Inhabit the higher shelves like an archduke. The
light in the fridge stays on when the door closes. Below you in the shuddering
machinery of cold, the fridge's crispy bowels, your so-called friends, your best
friends, forever save for you a chair; they like you to arrive riding two asses and
a bike.

Their voices skitter like scabies. In the backend all the addling algorithms riddle
red tracks like truth into your aching eyelids: We will melt you into the mysteries
like margarine, like the mayonnaise of modernity. We will circumcise you with
celery sticks and name you after the gastropod Golem. Your blood will slake our
veins like holy iodine.

Their pixelated wishes trickle down your most secret bioluminescent seas.
Your true head opens a heather-paved cave. They bury you in their ascent to
gory binary love. They link fingers to rasp iron filings and reach for the tear gas
canastas.

This time the subway

Rats—Don't Tolerate Them reads the subway station wall at midnight
you pay your fare at the unstaffed booth and glide down escalators
in the dim tunnel past the platform an unseen engine starts to drone
a breeze whispers along the platform picks up a wind turns a gale
forces commuters off their feet sucking them into the tunnel
they tumble like autumn leaves their phones shoes and loose
change clatter and smash on tile and stone they smear the tunnel red
ride the escalators watching others descend and vanish in the wind
you could do this all night but the fifth wind harvests you too
through the humid darkness round corners past maintenance crews
impervious in rail-clamping magnet boots and well paid for their silence
rush wide-eyed through the subway's underground maze
grit wires whiskers and tails lash your streaming face you ricochet
the tunnels' texture changing from sooty concrete to corrugated iron to
sandstone to carved marble to blood-slicked oesophagus to woven
mangrove roots amidst which swim blind white fish to a cavernous
ossuary lined with friezes rendered in femurs on its far wall gleams
and gnashes a steel-toothed shredder tall as a house you hurtle toward it
claw the walls grab at the lamps to stop flying at those interlocking
teeth filling the vast subterranean space with the smell of rust and oil
an alarm blares a shadow flashes you spot the kill switch panel
punch it miss it hear in some hidden alcove the engineer rats laughing
in the fraction of a second the teeth need to eat your arm you know
your bones won't even slow down the machine never mind jam it
as this marvel of modern transit and automatic malice roars towards you
know this—there's no kill switch for the city's romantic traffic in appetites
so lean in unhinge your jaw and kiss the engine's spinning indifferent teeth

Speeches for Francis Bacon's Three Studies for Figures at The Base of a Crucifixion

Chorus:

Come, visitor: let our three-winged tableau be your beacon. Come sear your gaze in our blaze of paint, beautiful as a maple leaf halved and flanked by gasping corpses. *All sorts of things happen all the time.* Come, hear us: we three queens, Eumenides, writhing on bare tables in barren orange cells, unhinging our jaws to welcome your spine. Hear our names: Alekto. Megaera. Tilphousia. We uncoil like sidewinders. We burn above you like suns hung from chains. We torrent rage from our square cages. We remember the book and its countless betrayals. Come, visitor: *Turn the key with the foot. Wander into the image.*

Says Alekto:

No, there was no fourth nail. But there was a fifth. No, I couldn't watch the red skulls rubble that hill for crows to gnaw. No, these aren't wings. No, I rode no Judas cradle: try the wretch next door. No, nobody in the bar saw him holding my throat. No, not my ashes. No, *I was born in Ireland, though my mother and father were both English.* No, thank you; the peels sting my chewed fingertips. No, I had nothing to do with the oak table. It's worth only a quarter. *It lives on its own.* No, you may not, absolutely not. No, I'm not crying. Why?

Spits Megaera:

Just you watch I'll cough bloody teeth up your nose you puke rat your tapeworm tongue needs a shave wait that posh prick minister pushing his bootstrap bull in here on all holiest of dais hell no do it while his smug fanny naps on the bench crushing the beetle republic of bleeding out you get how hard it gets *where two people tear each other apart you might just learn something using the meat the way one might use the spine* guards *guards* where are the fucking *guards* just you wait they'll take the piss out of you knock it back like gin they're always eating you always eating oh how I loved that show how the spear pierced and the water welled out oh how his mother shrieked like a boiling kettle wait no please don't go my bad mea culpa please help me get me off this thing I've been shitting blood for years

Soothes Tilphousia:

In the beginning, *there was a wide open city, which was very violent: out of pools of flesh rose specific people*. In the beginning they detained me for impersonating an elephant. They outlined my mouth in chalk. They fed me his soiled diaper. My sisters lie; Christ he was a horror, yellow pig with his throat slit. Naked, raining blood and urine. Naked, his teeth broken and knocked out. They arrested me crying on the bank of the Rhine. They sat me on these nails. They charged me with blasphemy by flowerpot. They sectioned me with a rust-clotted saw. They took me to the movie. They won. If I hold my mouth open, the rains will come, quench my thirst like salt slakes a slug. Quiet, now. The dead sun sinks. I hear thunder beyond this fruitless room. Come, rains. In someone else's heaven the lawnmowers all sleep. They forced my confession with tongs. They branded my tongue with the obligatory apology. No song but the Gnostic apocrypha told of the whores on that hill of skulls, how with thunder perfect minds they rose up and tore apart the scarab-faced guards. Quiet, now. *Feel a chance escaping*. Come, rains.

Chorus:

For the sunburn, you're welcome. Our ashen faces are now your face too. *Beautiful meat. To want the person reflected in the glass is illogical. The rooms at the back were all curved. Nothing is going to come.* May Pimlico's grey rains fan you, as you leave our altar, like crepitating fronds of desiccated palm. But we will never leave you: welcome us, your new sisters, like a balm for your peripheral vision. May the krill-rich sky over Angel Tube blacken under our shibboleths of weightless flesh. You're welcome. Go. *Work on the hazard that has been left to you: the mouth, its colour and the screaming.* All the crows in the bare black branches scream too, for now they are a law, Lazarus, as are you.

Nightmares in the university's ruins

1. Sessional twister

it's precarious work evading tornadoes
from clouds over the Qu'appelle Valley ridge
dirty black twisters reach down writhe and surge
toward the prairie farm house where you
shelter with your wife and toddler daughters

in the west one funnel hooks down from the clouds
like the tentacle of a giant furious kraken
then through the kitchen window you watch
more form on the eastern ridge so it's time
to punch in and scramble down to the basement

it's barely a crawlspace under the floorboards
with no headroom to sit upright no bedroom to hide in
never mind check your email or complete timesheets
the girls play like it's a game hiding under blankets
you squint through the boards worried where your next

paycheque's coming from and whether they'll question
the hours you've put in for including the hour you
needed to complete the paperwork properly and how
much pay they'll grind away like the funnel up there
grinds away the house above the hollering floorboards

through the cracks the gale needles grit into your skin
tell everyone to lie down flat and close their eyes
nothing for it now but to pad your resumé resign yourself
to the full time job hunt expecting only that soon twisters
will touch down long enough to earn names like hurricanes

2. Tenure track of the living dead

it's a full time career fleeing zombies
while the conference carries on nail shut the bunker
equip it with rations and citations for the coming winter
inside hands raise to offer lectures disguised as questions
outside hands grasp and teeth gnash to grind flesh

your weary ragtag research network sticks to waterways
wide abandoned malls and grant writing workshops
crosses the blood-flooded acropolises of old academe
climbs a rope ladder up through the library's glass floor
toils in small groups like the worst kind of homework

you review the terms and conditions with your colleagues
critique the carefully crafted applications they submit
check the credentials that prove they live
assess their annual performance according to rank
ensure they're not about to succumb about to turn

you need the student associations on your side to dispatch
the undead who keep on your cogently argued case
they swim dissolving after you they swarm the dorms
you advise your rising star grad student to revise and resubmit
set a firm deadline for the defence against infection seminar

the dean seconds you to the campus torture chambers
where the provost processes student bodies for export
where reanimation-centred budgeting dictates the hard decisions
now you know but you signed the nondisclosure agreement
they won't let you live but they will promote you to associate

Stranger music

we met in the agreed-on
school parking lot
in a far-off neighbourhood
neither of us lived in
she handed me the money
I handed her the violin
neither of us knew how to play
we drove away in opposite
directions leaving the lot like
no cars had ever parked there

Ecstasy, Euphrasia

still you stand
on the snow-coated, rye-stubbled hillside
above the farmhouse where your high school
friends are starting the bottle count, the blare
of grunge, the making of pasta from scratch

still you stand alone in the ice-crusted snow
of New Year's Eve 1990
a Cowboy Junkies song stuck in your head
your body for my soul fair swap
when this sight stalls your senses:

all the hills of Beaver Valley huddle together like sheep
too old and asleep to mind how the slow knife
of seasons shears their backs
where the hills' noses nudge one another
runs the winter-burnt thicket of the Beaver River
crosshatched by the black leafless branches of alders
that shelter the cold shack of the Grey County gun club

fields quilted by fence posts pin old houses to the old map
of faded flags, weathered walls, wind-bent slant, and
unravelled ribbons of gravel concessions
in those centenarian homes
an apple farmer drowns kittens by the handful
a kitchen fills with back issues
a mother dies in a bed in a yellow bedroom
and yard-stranded trailers await spring's migrant hands

a far highway bisects the valley in a northward line
to the turbid horizon of Georgian Bay
traversed by a caravan of miniature minivans bound
for downhill powder and broken legs in the Blue Mountains
on the western ridge, a barn roof blazons our owl-kill flag
snow-coated emus stalk the pasture, talking
in their hushed drum tongue

the pine and maple trunks touched with orange paint
point the Bruce Trail to Thomson's unknown tomb

down the side road, an abandoned house, open as a shirt
across its frostbitten floor spills a mouldy library:
sepia softcore postcards, true crime pulp
a first edition of *Earth's Enigmas*

a tiding of crows rides the midwinter thermals
their barks bounce off the drowsing hills
draw your eye to the grey flannel sky
buttoned by a cottonball sun
that whispers *you are happy*

your breath brakes on the noise of this new signal
as you come down the hill where you still and will
always stand, awake and oblivious
only now do you know what the sun says is true
and only later do you know it is true
this moment wraps you like a Moebius strip ever after

for years crawl blindly around these rye stalks
feeling for the eye you dropped here beside yourself
retrace your tracks, rewrite the scene a dozen ways
as a diptych in acrylics, as a mixtape of lost songs
I'm thinking about mortality
it's a cheap price we pay for existence
as an arrangement for choir and pipes, as a honeybees' dance
as one too many tokes over the scorched timeline
as this poem

pour whole days like today into trying to say it
still nothing fixes this spot of time that
always has existed, always will exist
pointing like a compass through choice and chance
through your blood's blind drift
towards what it wants not knowing what it wants

but is what the sun says true just as a riddle
or does it point to some plan deep and long as a shadow
still to come from history's blizzard
in this ravenous new century only
hindsight will illuminate like the waste
witnessed by that storm-battered angel
he would like to pause for a moment so fair

maybe what the sun says must stay unsaid
out of time abiding gravid to spawn synaptic
sparks like cloud lightning
across an overcast life, leaking from a street
corner, a radio song, a crow's flight

from her smile seen underwater
from the chasm ink opens into the page
whenever you write or
merely remember you want to
but the impetus turns to impasse and arrests you
but I hold all this to myself

so for now, then, which is always now
just carry this moment since from now on it carries you:
not a penny to press in your pocket
but a never-healing, poppy-red tattoo

In Gwen MacEwen Park

three oaks and three chestnuts sentinel this oasis
kids caper in the nearby schoolyard
sparrows ricochet around Walmer Baptist
an ant traverses my shirt
a robin wades through the unweeded grass

women cross the park with varied charges
a baby a baguette a book
they pass the plinth with MacEwen's head
above an engraved quotation from *Afterworlds*
—we are still dancing, dancing—

in a city forever on fastforward
taxis circle the park's three stop signs
at the park's south end stand two new saplings
one a slim magnolia planted last year
in Connie Rooke's memory

the reason I've come here
under the magnolia a plaque commemorates
Connie's open-heart theory
*—the act of writing holds out the promise
of an ever-deepening connection to the heart of life—*

I splash a dram from my cup onto the sunwarm soil
recall her talk about *invoking the you*
Connie you were all heart with my writing back then
is it too late to tell you I've found it again
to say thank you for the eternal bright light

I want to stay in this chestnut shade
let more ants traverse my shirt
but I have to get back to the conference
where new poets sharp as scalpels will be reading
I will try to listen with a heart open as Kahlo's

over the church storm clouds thicken in gridlock
I walk to the subway posting a photo
in my socials a friend who knew Connie too says
that park is like the Secret Garden
surrounded by a wall of city streets

Cash paradise

A day after our seventeenth anniversary, we sipped coffee on the backyard patio,
my mug the one I'd stolen from work, hers the one she'd designed, quoting the kids.
Above us the high sheltering hands of the elms laced their green fingers together,
magpies whined like machines winding up, and the resident wrens warbled and burble
The air above that canopy or bower burned purely cloudlessly azure and
the myriad engines of the neighbours all still slept mute as winter in their garages.
On her phone she pored over the registry for a cousin's wedding we're going to. "Wha
about bed linens?" I said we should get those for the couple if they'd hang them
out the window after the wedding night, "because tradition." I was puzzling over the
weekend paper's crossword poetry—girl from Glasgow: *lass*; psychic glows: *aurae*;
hearing-based: *aural*; "haven't you been listening to me": *hello*—but I had been listenin
riffing—as her laughter testified—and recalling Johnny Cash's answer to *Vanity Fair's*
Proustian question—*When and where were you happiest?*—with six words that descri
us just at that sonnet of a post-solstice moment: *this morning, having coffee, with her.*

Moon of a far planet

a dim egg-blue moon looms low in the subarctic sky
cloudless and free for once of the haze breezing in
from the boreal blazes this spring evening

you amble back from the corner store
wondering for the nth time why you moved across the country
to work from home in this alien northern town

that faint nail clip moon looks like a movie poster moon
like an airbrushed cliché anchored above a far planet's
violet sky opulent with constellations

a planet where some dozen corpse-mongers
hoard more in their dead fists than the billions of the barely living
whose pockets vibrate and snitch on their whereabouts

a planet where ancient giant insects still hunt
among the soft-shelled refugees from the latest Ice Age
a planet whose skies writhe with ghost lights each night

a planet where soldiers storm homes to stop sharing
where funerals for music teachers feature no music
where only barest scrutiny gets held to dead cities

a planet where the rate at which burned land
refreshes its green screen televises a promise
that even a fire can tell a vision

a planet where in the interminable winter you stud your shoes
with screws to walk ice coated streets with a hyper spaniel
a planet no weirder nor farther than anyone's prairie area code

with friends only close onscreen as forest fire smoke encroaches
to see the moon like this is to marvel and fear
how far our planet is from anything but our own devices

Fuseli in Peru

Down into the cloud-flannelled forest of the Inca Trail
You fly supine and feet first, as if you ride a luge sled
Fly to Dead Woman's Pass
Land below the sandal-worn saddle of the pass
See the top of an evergreen approaching the pass
From the other side of the mountain, unknown as night
The evergreen comes into focus astride a horse
Watch this horse as it careens towards you
And as if you ride it too
Gripping only its sweat-slicked mane for reins
Mark this horse as it crests the pass
Hooves hammering the root-veined earth

Figure what comes here

The horse careens over the pass, frothing
It is not a whole horse galloping
Only the front half of a horse severed from its hind
Its mad eyes rolling
The half-horse barrels toward you, like a stage costume falling apart
Tumbling entrails not clowns

Figure what comes here

Figure what first appeared above the saddle of the pass
A red-branched conifer, saddling the horse
No—impaling the horse
A fearful symmetry of red branches stakes its spine
As if this mare has sprouted a second spine out its skin
As this horse charges you, momentum its only world now

Its unbearable conifer tilts and shivers like a standard
It bears you news of the new chaos
Imminent as breath
Inescapable as rain

Notes

Taking things without giving credit always relates to a history of colonialism.

—Jacob Wren, Facebook post (2017)

Acker uses dreams as another means of relinquishing authorial control over the writing and returning to one of the original functions of the early cut-up, namely to bring writing closer to the subconscious mind.

—Edward Robinson, "From Cut-Up to Cut and Paste, Plagiarism and Adaptation: Kathy Acker's Evolution of Burroughs and Gysin's Cut-Up Technique" (2010)

Whether copied in substantial or insubstantial part, expression that creates and conveys meaning constitutes a legitimate exercise of freedom of expression.

—Bita Amani, "Copyright and Freedom of Expression"

All uses of quotation and excerpting in this book adhere to the Center for Media and Social Impact's *Code of Best Practices in Fair Use for Poetry* (http://cmsimpact.org/code/code-best-practices-fair-use-poetry/).

"Shadows the words"

This cento, which is also an acrostic, consists of one line taken from each of the following poems (in order of appearance): Kathleen Ossip's "Your Ardor"; Philip Schultz's "Afterwards"; Sarah Eliza Johnson's "Combustion"; "Noelle Kocot's "On being an artist"; Philip Levine's "Our Valley"; Adam Clay's "Our Daily Becoming"; and Julia Cohen's "In the dark we crush."

"Three votive candles"
The poem's subsection titles excerpt and adapt phrases from the biblical New Testament.

"Here is where was"
The line *"what lips it had were tattered and bloody"* is from Basil Johnston's *The Manitous: The Spiritual World of the Ojibway* (Minnesota Historical Society, 2001); the line *"where is here"* is from Northrop Frye's 1965 "Conclusion to the First Edition of *Literary History of Canada*" (in *Northrop Frye on Canada*, vol. 12, edited by Jean O'Grady and David Staines, University of Toronto Press, 2003); and the line *"Here was beauty and here was nowhere"* is from Dionne Brand's *No Language is Neutral* (Coach House Press, 1990).

"Second of the night"
The poem's title quotes Heart's "These dreams" (Capitol, 1986).

"No family one pictures"
This cento is composed of excerpts from my great-aunt Ella Kittmer's unpublished typescript "The Kittmer Family Tree," written circa 1970, and from Walter Benjamin's "Theses on the Philosophy of History" (*Illuminations*, translated by Hannah Arendt, Schocken, 1969).

"Take forever just a minute"
The poem's title and its fourth-from-last line is from the Bee Gees' "More Than a Woman" (RSO, 1977).

"A pantoum to smash pandas"
The second (and fifth) line is from "Da Mystery of Chessboxin'" by the Wu Tang Clan (Loud, 1993). PANDAS stands for Pediatric Autoimmune Neuropsychiatric Disorders Associated with Streptococcal Infections; it is diagnosed when a child exhibits obsessive compulsive disorder (OCD) or tic symptoms that appear suddenly, or worsen drastically, following an infection such as strep throat or scarlet fever (for more information, see NIMH's "PANDAS—Questions and Answers" at https://www.nimh.nih.gov/health/publications/pandas/index.shtml).

"Anthropocene obscene as orange"

The line *"the cities wash away"* is excerpted from the lyrics of R.E.M.'s "So. Central Rain (I'm Sorry)" (IRS, 1984). The line *"eye of the hurricane listen"* is from R.E.M.'s "It's the End of the World As We Know It (And I Feel Fine)" (IRS, 1987). "New Orleans is sinking" refers to the eponymous song by The Tragically Hip (MCA, 1989). The phrase "smoke-smuggered sky" is from Dr. Seuss' *The Lorax* (Random House, 1971).

"Room for one more"

The poem's title refers to the recurring phrase in "Twenty Two," episode 53 of *The Twilight Zone* (CBS, 10 February 1961).

"Mab and Burke"

For no mere mortal can resist and "the funk of forty thousand years" are quoted from Michael Jackson's "Thriller" (Thriller, Epic/CBS, 1982).

"L'âme de l'homme est fait du papier"

"L'âme de l'homme est fait du papier" ("The human soul is made of paper") is a phrase from Michel Tournier's 1970 novel *Le Roi des aulnes* (*The Erl-King*).

"Voyager 2, thinking, types things"

This cento (and sonnet) is composed of excerpted tweets by @NSFVoyager2. The poem's title adapts that of "Thinking Voyager 2 Types Things" by Bob Geldof (Atlantic, 1990).

"Lunar sonata"

This cento is composed of selectively excerpted phrases from "Audio recordings document 'weird music' heard by Apollo astronauts on far side of moon," by Lee Speigel (*Huffington Post*, 20 February 2016).

"Heaven help the roses"

The poem's title is a line from Stevie Wonder's song "Heaven help us all" (Motown, 1970). The Benjamin quotation in lines 44–45 is from "Theses on the philosophy of history" (*Illuminations*, translated by Hannah Arendt, Shocken, 1969).

"Forgive me Cathy for"
The line "I have been contemplating suicide but it really doesn't suit my style" is from "Shivers" by the Boys Next Door (Mushroom, 1979). The lines "I have always found myself determined to survive" and "I have suddenly realized the meaning of *My Mother: Demonology*" are from Kathy Acker's novel *My Mother: Demonology* (Grove Press, 1993). Some lines and phrases (like "I have to be in heaven"; "wick slip", "I have a right to kiss her", and "I have lost the locket") are from Emily Brontë's *Wuthering Heights* (1847). "I have come home let me / have it" are phrases borrowed from Kate Bush's 1978 song "Wuthering Heights" (EMI, 1977).

"The lineaments"
The first stanza adapts William Blake's *Notebook* poem no. 41 (1793).

"New patriot love"
The poem's title and several lines adapt the lyrics of the national anthem "O Canada." "owl kill in snow" is from Margaret Atwood's *Cat's Eye* (McClelland & Stewart, 1988).

"Shape your eyes by shutting them"
This poem (like this book) takes its title from a line in André Breton and Paul Éluard's *The Immaculate Conception*, translated by Jon Graham (Atlas Press, 1990).

"Was I asleep?"
The italicized phrase in the third stanza is from William Shakespeare's *King Lear*; the line *"When you sit with meat you rot"* is something my younger child said when ten years old.

"The Pit of Carkoon"
"The Pit of Carkoon" is a setting, and "the sarlacc" its resident monster, in the film *Return of the Jedi* (Lucasfilm 1985).

"Raver in the bathroom"
The poem's title adapts The English Beat's "Mirror in the bathroom" (Go Feet, 1980). The phrase *a city for a night* is from Frank Brewster and Bill Broughton's *Last Night a DJ Saved My Life: The History of the Disc Jockey* (Headline 2006).

"Like opening your refrigerator door"
The epigraph is from Dani Fankhauser's article "18 Facebook fossils we'll remember forever" in *Mashable* (25 January 2013).

"Speeches for Francis Bacon's Figures at the Base of a Crucifixion"
The title refers to Francis Bacon's painting *Three Studies for Figures at the Base of a Crucifixion* (1944). Italicized phrases quote Bacon's statements in David Sylvester's *The Brutality of Fact* (Thames & Hudson, 1975).

"Nightmares in the university's ruins"
The poem engages with Bill Readings' book *The University in Ruins* (Harvard University Press, 1996).

"Stranger music"
The poem borrows its title from Leonard Cohen's *Stranger Music: Selected Poems and Songs* (McClelland & Stewart, 1993).

"Ecstasy, Euphrasia"
The lines *your body for my soul fair swap* and *but I hold all this to myself* are from "'Cause cheap is how I feel" by Cowboy Junkies (RCA, 1990). "Owl-kill" as a simile for the Canadian flag is from Margaret Atwood's *Cat's Eye* (McClelland & Stewart, 1988). *I'm thinking about mortality* and *it's a cheap price we pay for existence* are lines from "Thinking Voyager 2 Type Things" by Bob Geldof (Atlantic, 1990). The line *always has existed, always will exist* is from Kurt Vonnegut's *Slaughterhouse-Five* (Delacorte, 1969), and *he would like to pause for a moment so fair* is from Walter Benjamin's "Theses on the Philosophy of History" (*Illuminations*, translated by Hannah Arendt, Schocken, 1969).

"In Gwen MacEwen Park"

The poem quotes monuments in Gwendolyn MacEwen Park that quote from MacEwen's poem "Late Song" (*Afterworlds*, McClelland & Stewart, 1987) and from Constance Rooke's introduction to *Writing Life* (McClelland & Stewart, 2006).

"Cash paradise"

The poem quotes from Johnny Cash's "Proust Questionnaire" interview with *Vanity Fair* (as quoted on the magazine's website at https://www.vanityfair.com/culture/2009/11/proust-book-200911).

Acknowledgements and publication credits

Several of the poems included in this book were first published by the following journals and organizations, to which I am very grateful. I am also deeply thankful to the teachers, mentors, and colleagues with whom I workshopped many of the poems in this collection; to the manuscript's anonymous reviewers for their tough, incisive, and generous feedback; to everyone at AU Press; and to Peter Midgley, who edited the collection and helped it achieve its final form.

"Shadows the words" was first published in *UnLost*, 4 June 2017.

"Three votive candles" was first published in an earlier version in *subTerrain*, no. 28, 2000, pp. 27–28.

"Here is where was" was first published in *Existere*, vol. 35, no. 2, 2016, p. 21.

"No family one pictures" was first published in an earlier version in *EVENT Magazine*, vol. 46, 2017, pp. 48–49.

"Grand parenthesis" was first published in an earlier version in *The Eramosa Anthology*, edited by Katherine L. Gordon and Joshua Willoughby, Eramosa Writers Group, 1996, pp. 72–73.

"A sound outside the house" and "Was I asleep?" were first accepted for publication in *Coffin Bell*, vol. 2, no. 3, 2019, in press.

"The leaf is not the line" earned Honourable Mention in *Riddle Fence*'s 2017 Compton Poetry Contest and was first published in *Riddle Fence*, no. 28, 2017, pp. 22–23.

"Why the blue whale risked its neck" was first published in *On Spec Magazine*, vol. 29, no. 1, 2018, p. 49.

"Mab and Burke" was first published in an earlier version in *subTerrain*, no. 21, 1996, p. 31.

"Voyager 2, thinking, types things" was first published in *concīs*, Winter 2017, https://concis.io/issues/winter-2017/mark-a-mccutcheon-voyager-2/.

"Lunar sonata" was first published in *Tigershark ezine*, no. 11, 2016, p. 9.

"Baby Bee explains Jupiter's Great Red Spot" and "The Pit of Carkoon" were first published in earlier versions in *Writual*, no. 2, 1995, pp. 25–26.

"Heaven help the roses" earned Runner-Up in *Into the Void*'s 2017 Poetry Contest, and was first published in *Into the Void* online, 21 January 2018, https://intothevoidmagazine.com/2017-winners/.

"The lineaments" was first published in *Quills*, no. XI, pp. 52–53.

"New patriot love" was first published in *Milkweed Zine*, no. 3, Spring 2017, pp. 41–42.

"The space of one paragraph" was first published in *Riddled With Arrows*, vol. 2, no. 2, 2018, http://www.riddledwitharrows.com/riddled-with-arrows-issue-2-2-toc/shadow-play/#space.

"Stranger music" was shortlisted for the Edmonton Poetry Festival and Edmonton Transit Service's Poetry Moves on Transit contest in 2018, and was first published on the Edmonton Poetry Festival's shortlist website, on 13 June 2018, http://edmontonpoetryfestival.com/poetry-route/.

"Cash paradise" was first published in *Grain*, vol. 46, no. 1, 2018, p. 72.

"Moon of a far planet" was first published in *Star*Line*, vol. 41, no. 4, Fall 2018, p. 37.

"Fuseli in Peru" was first published in *Kaleidotrope*, April 2014, http://www.kaleidotrope.net/archives/spring-2014-2/fuseli-in-peru-by-mark-a-mccutcheon/.